12/18 2008

EXPLORING

VENUS

Published in 2018 by
KidHaven Publishing, an Imprint of Greenhaven Publishing, LLC
353 3rd Avenue
Suite 255
New York, NY 10010

Designer: Deanna Paternostro
Editor: Vanessa Oswald

Photo credits: Cover, back cover, p. 17 (background) Vadim Sadovski/Shutterstock.com; p. 5 Naeblys/Shutterstock.com; p. 7 Irina Kuzmina/Shutterstock.com; p. 9 NASA images/ Shutterstock.com; p. 11 Jcpag2012/Wikimedia Commons; p. 13 SCIEPRO/Getty Images; p. 15 Space Frontiers/Stringer/Archive Photos/Getty Images; p. 17 reziart/Shutterstock.com; pp. 18–19 Everett Historical/Shutterstock.com; p. 21 SteinsplittlerBot/Wikimedia Commons.

Cataloging-in-Publication Data

Names: Beckett, Leslie.
Title: Exploring Venus / Leslie Beckett .
Description: New York : KidHaven Publishing, 2018. | Series: Journey through our solar system | Includes index.
Identifiers: ISBN 9781534522879 (pbk.) | 9781534522732 (library bound) | ISBN 9781534522589 (6 pack) | ISBN 9781534522596 (ebook)
Subjects: LCSH: Venus (Planet)–Juvenile literature.
Classification: LCC QB621.B3935 2018 | DDC 523.42–dc23
Printed in the United States of America

CPSIA compliance information: Batch #BS17KL: For further information contact Greenhaven Publishing LLC, New York, New York at 1-844-317-7404.

CONTENTS

THE BRIGHTEST PLANET

Venus is the brightest planet in the **solar system** and the second planet from the sun. It can be seen in the night sky without a **telescope**. The moon is the only object in the sky that's brighter.

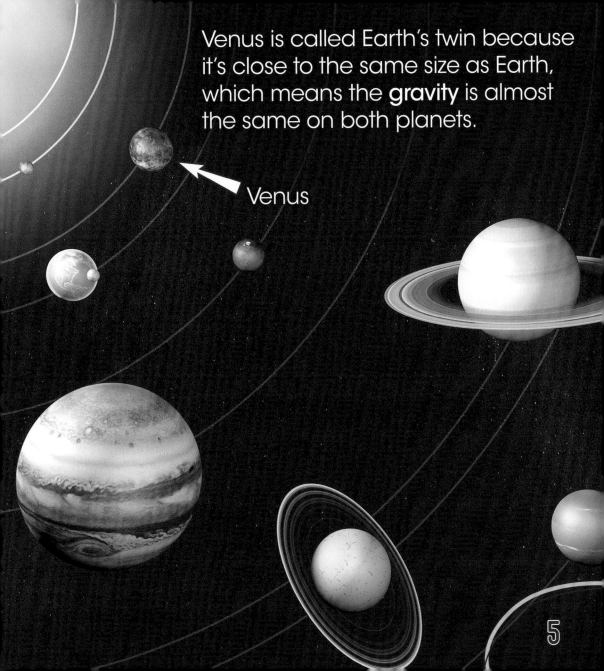

Venus is called Earth's twin because it's close to the same size as Earth, which means the **gravity** is almost the same on both planets.

Venus

Venus appears in the sky most often just before sunrise and just after sunset. It has been called the Morning Star and the Evening Star.

moon

Venus

Venus is one of
the brightest space
objects in the sky.

SLOW MOVER

Venus spins around more slowly than any other planet. It takes the planet 243 Earth days to make a full spin, or rotation. It also spins in the opposite direction from most of the other planets.

The only other planet that spins in the same direction as Venus is Uranus.

Venus **orbits** the sun just like all the other planets. The planet takes 225 Earth days to orbit the sun. The only planet with a faster orbit around the sun is Mercury.

The sun rises in the west and sets in the east on Venus. This is the opposite of Earth.

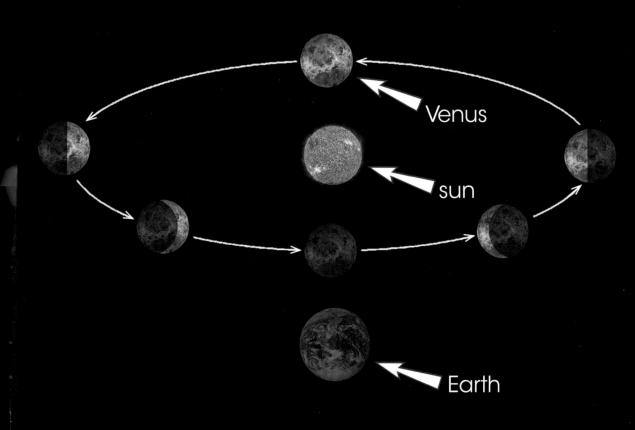

Venus

sun

Earth

IN THE CLOUDS OF VENUS

Venus is covered in thick clouds made up of harmful gases such as carbon dioxide and sulfuric acid. These clouds hide the planet and are very different from Earth's clouds.

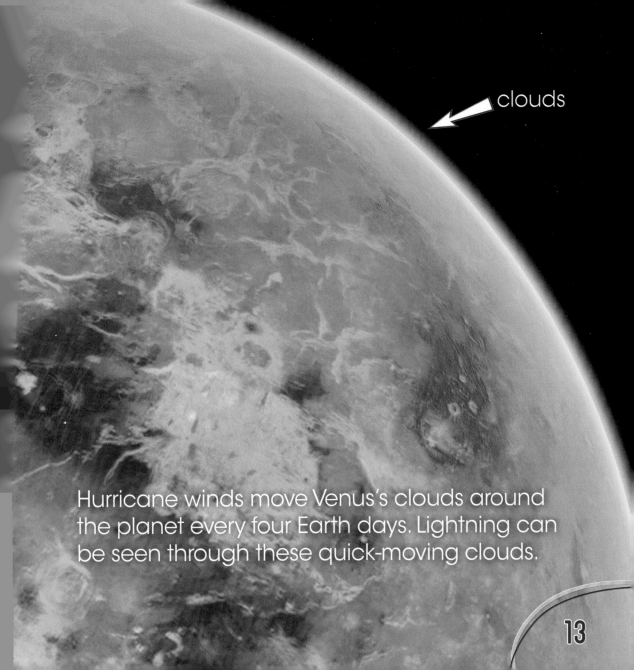

clouds

Hurricane winds move Venus's clouds around the planet every four Earth days. Lightning can be seen through these quick-moving clouds.

The clouds on Venus trap the sun's heat. This makes Venus the hottest planet in the solar system. It can get hotter than 880 degrees Fahrenheit (470 degrees Celsius) on Venus!

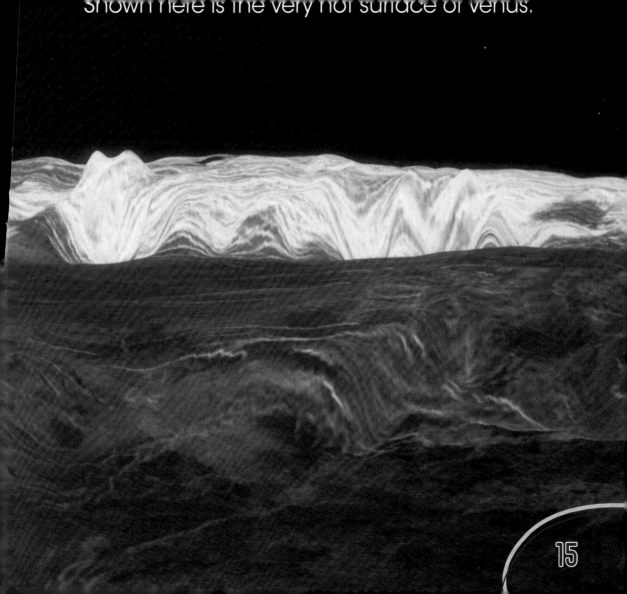

Shown here is the very hot surface of Venus.

15

UNDERNEATH THE CLOUDS

Venus's ground is made of rock. Beneath the ground is a hot, rocky **mantle**. The mantle sometimes moves. This makes the ground above it move and creates **volcanoes**. The core, or center of the planet, is made of iron.

carbon dioxide

Venus's clouds and hot, rocky mantle make it the hottest planet.

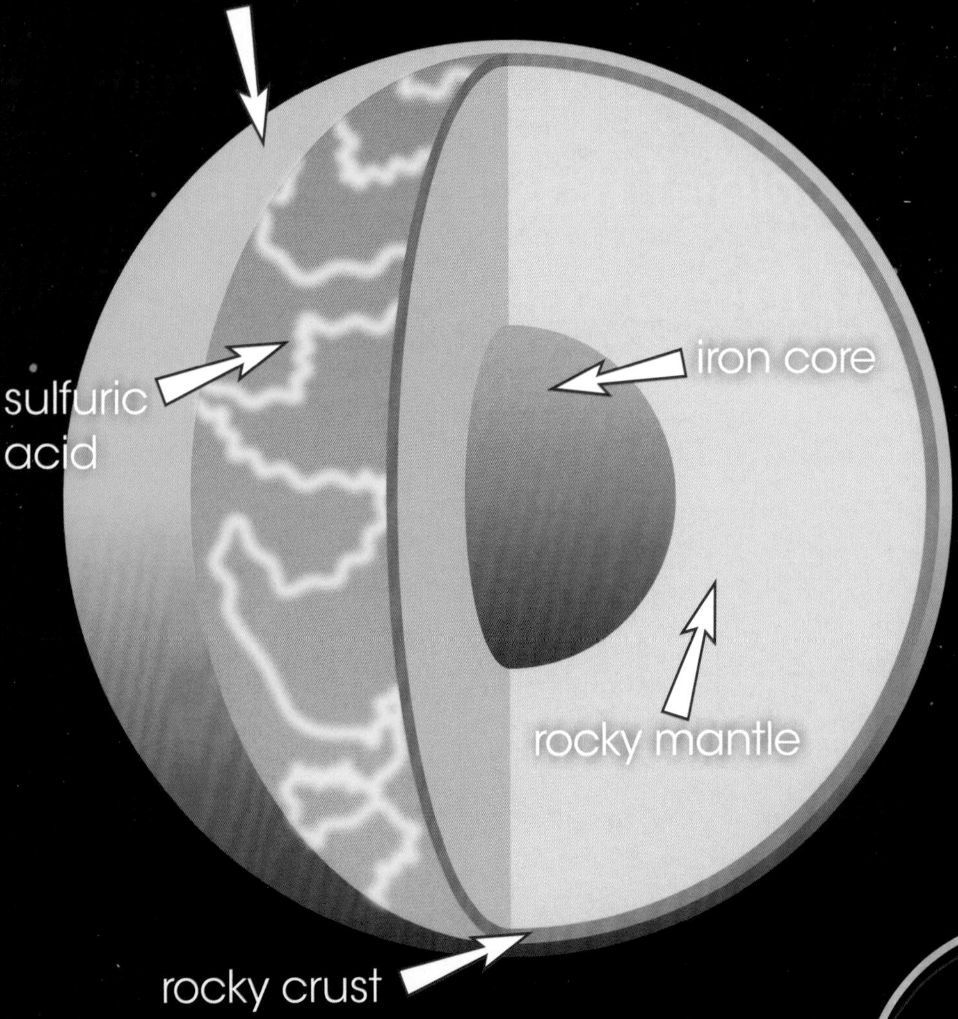

sulfuric acid

iron core

rocky mantle

rocky crust

Venus is covered with mountains, **plains, craters,** and volcanoes. The planet has more than 1,600 large volcanoes.

The highest mountain on Venus is Maxwell Montes, which is 20,000 feet (6.1 km) high. This is almost as high as Mount Everest, which is Earth's highest mountain.

Venus has more volcanoes than any other planet in the solar system. However, most of them are **dormant**.

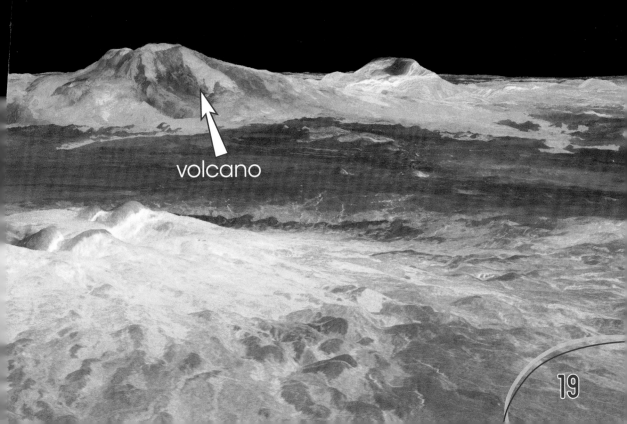

volcano

STUDYING VENUS

Many **probes** have been sent to Venus to find out more about the planet. In 1962, *Mariner 2* reached Venus and discovered its hot temperatures. It was the first probe to send back information from another planet.

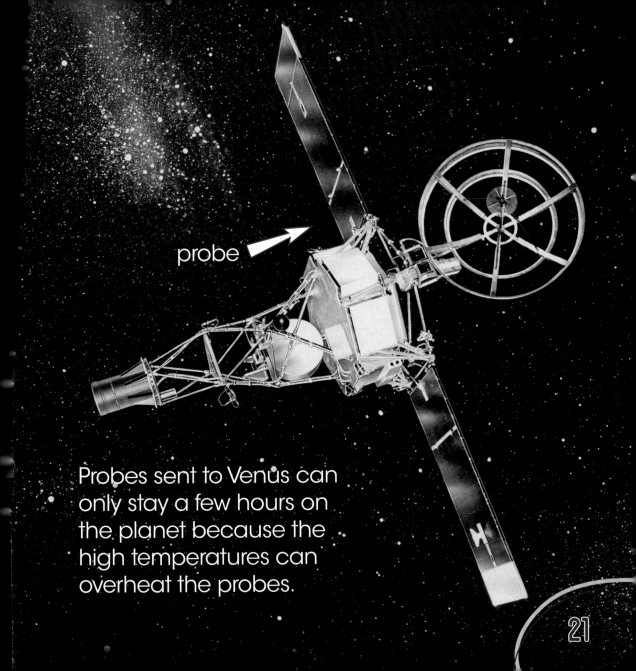

probe

Probes sent to Venus can
only stay a few hours on
the planet because the
high temperatures can
overheat the probes.

GLOSSARY

crater: A large, bowl-shaped hole found on the surface of a planet or moon.

dormant: Not active.

gravity: The force that makes all things with mass move toward one another.

mantle: The part of a planet underneath the ground.

orbit: To travel in a circle or oval around something.

plain: A large area of flat land.

probe: A vehicle that sends information about an object in space back to Earth.

solar system: The sun and all the space objects that orbit it, including the planets and their moons.

telescope: An instrument used to view distant objects, such as the planets in space.

volcano: An opening in a planet's surface through which hot, liquid rock sometimes flows.

FOR MORE INFORMATION

Websites

NASA: All About Venus
spaceplace.nasa.gov/all-about-venus/en/
This website features pictures of and fun facts about Venus.

National Geographic Kids: Mission to Venus
kids.nationalgeographic.com/explore/space/ mission-to-venus/#venus-planet.jpg
Visitors to this website can take a closer look at the hottest planet.

Books

Berne, Emma Carlson. *The Secrets of Venus.* North Mankato, MN: Capstone Press, 2016.

Bloom, J.P. *Venus.* Minneapolis, MN: ABDO Kids, 2015.

Roumanis, Alexis. *Venus.* New York, NY: AV2 by Weigl, 2016.

INDEX